Kenya

by Barbara Saffer

Content Consultant:
David Sandgren
Professor of African History, Concordia College
Moorhead, Minnesota
Reading Consultant:
Dr. Robert Miller, Professor of Special Education
Minnesota State University, Mankato

Bridgestone Books
an imprint of Capstone Press
Mankato, Minnesota

Bridgestone Books are published by Capstone Press
151 Good Counsel Drive, P.O. Box 669, Mankato, Minnesota 56002
http://www.capstone-press.com

Library of Congress Cataloging-in-Publication Data
Saffer, Barbara.
    Kenya/by Barbara Saffer.
    p. cm.—(Countries and cultures)
    Includes bibliographical references (p. 61) and index.
    ISBN 0-7368-0771-3
    1. Kenya—Juvenile literature. [1. Kenya.] I. Title. II. Series.
DT433.522 .S24 2002
967.62—dc21   00-009833

Summary: An introduction to the geography, history, economy, culture,
    and people of Kenya.

Editorial Credits

Connie R. Colwell and Gillia M. Olson, editors; Lois Wallentine, product
    planning editor; Heather Kindseth, designer; Heidi Meyer, illustrator;
    Katy Kudela, photo researcher

Photo Credits

Bruce Coleman, Inc., 18; Capstone Press/Gary Sundermeyer, 53; David
Sandgren, 1 (right), 23, 42, 48, 50–51; Digital Stock, 63; Gary W. Sargent, 13;
Jason Lauré, 4, 28, 54, 56; Joe McDonald/TOM STACK & ASSOCIATES, 31;
John Shaw/TOM STACK & ASSOCIATES, cover (right); McDonald Wildlife
Photography, 20, 41; One Mile Up, Inc., 57 (both); PhotoDisc, Inc., 1 (left),
16–17; Photosphere, 45; Spencer Swanger/TOM STACK & ASSOCIATES, 15;
Tom & Pat Leeson, cover (left); TRIP/N. Jacobs, 8; TRIP/T. Bognar, 32;
TRIP/E. Wedo, 34; TRIP/L. Reemer, 46; Visuals Unlimited/Will Froyer, 1
(center), 24; W. Perry Conway/TOM STACK & ASSOCIATES, 26

Artistic Effects

Capstone Press, Digital Vision, PhotoDisc, Inc.

1 2 3 4 5 6 07 06 05 04 03 02

Contents

Fast Facts about Kenya

Name: Jamhuri ya Kenya; Republic of Kenya

Location: eastern Africa

Bordering countries and bodies of water: Ethiopia, Sudan, Uganda, Tanzania, Somalia, and the Indian Ocean

National population: 30,339,770

Capital: Nairobi

Major cities and populations: Nairobi (2,310,000); Mombasa (600,000); Kisumu (201,000); Nakuru (124,000); Kericho (11,000)

Explore Kenya

The African nation of Kenya is home to one of the world's largest wild animal reserves. Tsavo National Park stretches across more than 8,000 square miles (20,720 square kilometers) in eastern Kenya. Springs, low trees, grasslands, and water holes cover Tsavo.

Thousands of different types of animals roam the park. Crocodiles and hippos live in water holes. Elephants, zebras, and rhinos feed on grasses and plants, while giraffes munch on tree leaves. Predators such as lions, leopards, and cheetahs prowl through tall grasses. Herds of gazelles and antelopes leap across the park's plains. Hundreds of types of birds fly overhead.

The Nairobi-Mombasa Highway and the Mombasa-Uganda Railroad cut through Tsavo National Park. Each year, thousands of tourists from around the world travel these major thoroughfares to the park. They take guided tours of Tsavo to view and

◀ A guide at Tsavo National Park observes an African elephant. Guides can approach animals they know are unlikely to attack.

photograph animals in their natural habitats. Through these safaris, or journeys, visitors can learn how some of the world's rarest animals live in the wild.

About Kenya

Tourists on safari in Kenya come to see more than just the amazing wildlife. Kenya's visitors can climb mountains, wander the plains, or swim in the ocean.

Kenya lies on the eastern coast of Africa. Ethiopia and Sudan border Kenya on the north. Uganda lies to the west. Tanzania stretches along Kenya's southwestern border. Somalia and the Indian Ocean form Kenya's eastern boundary. With an area of 224,960 square miles (582,650 square kilometers), Kenya is slightly smaller than the U.S. state of Texas.

A land of many cultures, Kenya also has one of the fastest-growing populations in the world. The nation's population increases by about 1.53 percent each year. In 1999, about 28 million people lived in Kenya. In 2000, the country's population stood at about 29 million.

In past years, Kenya's people were divided. Kenyans claimed membership in different ethnic groups. In recent years, many Kenyans have pushed for a national identity. They hope that by uniting as Kenyans, they will build a strong and independent nation.

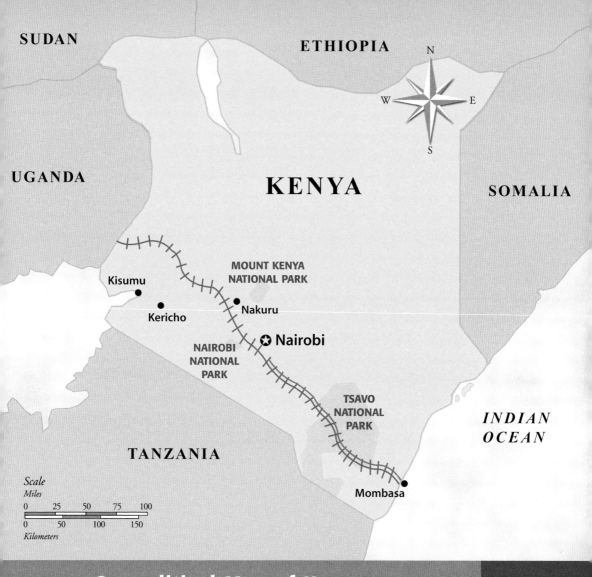

SUDAN

ETHIOPIA

N

W   E

S

UGANDA

KENYA

SOMALIA

Kisumu

MOUNT KENYA
NATIONAL PARK

Kericho

Nakuru

⊗ Nairobi

NAIROBI
NATIONAL
PARK

TSAVO
NATIONAL
PARK

INDIAN
OCEAN

TANZANIA

Scale
Miles

0   25   50   75   100

0   50   100   150

Kilometers

Mombasa

Geopolitical Map of Kenya

KEY

⊗ Capital

● Cities

▢ National Parks

✕╫ Mombasa-Uganda Railroad

▱ Nairobi-Mombasa Highway

7

Fast Facts about Kenya's Land

Area: 224,960 square miles (582,650 square kilometers)

Latitude and longitude: 1 degree north latitude, 38 degrees east longitude

Highest elevation: Mount Kenya, 17,058 feet (5,199 meters)

Lowest elevation: Indian Ocean, sea level

Chapter 2

The Land, Climate, and Wildlife

Kenya is a country of variety. Tall peaks, deep canyons, waving grasslands, and sandy beaches cover the land. Kenya can be divided into three geographic regions—the coast, the plains, and the highlands. Each region has its own landscape, climate, and wildlife.

The Coast

Kenya's coastal region stretches about 300 miles (480 kilometers) along the southeastern edge of the country. Here, Kenya's shoreline meets the waters of the Indian Ocean. The busy port of Mombasa is one of Kenya's coastal cities. Nearby islands also belong to Kenya's coastal region.

White, sandy beaches line Kenya's coast, and many lagoons lie offshore. These shallow pools of seawater are separated from the ocean by narrow strips of land. Coconut palms, teak trees, and sandalwood trees grow

◀ Indian Ocean waters lap against Kenya's white, sandy beaches.

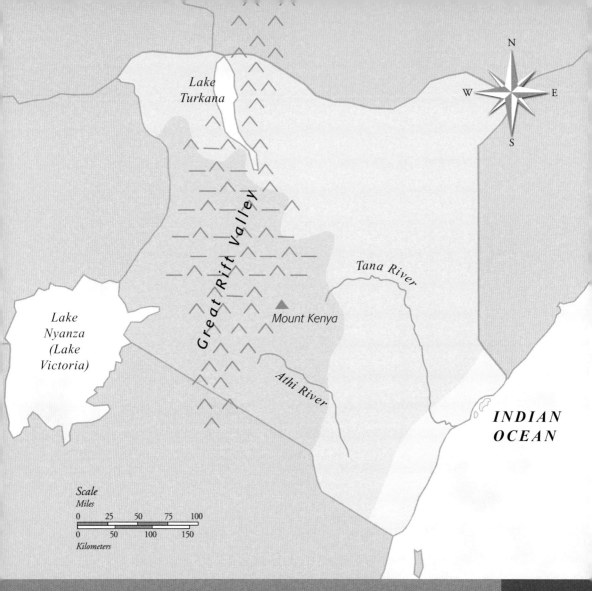

Lake
Turkana

Great Rift Valley

Lake
Nyanza
(Lake
Victoria)

Mount Kenya

Tana River

Athi River

*INDIAN
OCEAN*

N
W   E
S

Scale
Miles
0   25   50   75   100
0   50   100   150
Kilometers

Kenya's Land Regions and Topography

KEY

Highlands

Plains

Coast

Mountain

Mountain Ranges

Rivers

along Kenya's beaches and farther inland.

Many rivers and streams empty into the ocean from Kenya's coastal region. Kenya's longest river, the Tana, flows from central Kenya to the coast. Swampland borders some of the rivers.

A variety of wildlife lives in Kenya's coastal area. The lagoons are home to hippos and crocodiles. Tropical fish, such as barracuda, marlins, and yellowfin tuna, swim in the ocean waters near the coast. Many types of birds and butterflies also live in this region.

Kenya's coastal region is hot and humid year-round. The average temperature is 80 degrees Fahrenheit (27 degrees Celsius). The region receives an average of 40 inches (102 centimeters) of rain each year.

The Plains

Kenya's plains lie north and west beyond the coast. The plains region, also called the savanna, covers about two-thirds of Kenya. This grassland slopes upward in elevation from sea level to more than 3,000 feet (914 meters) high.

The plains region is cooler and drier than the coast. In the low altitudes of the east, the average temperature is 80 degrees Fahrenheit (27 degrees Celsius). In higher elevations, temperatures generally are cooler. The northern and western plains are dry, receiving an average of less than 10 inches (25 centimeters) of rain per year. The rest of the plains region sees an average of 30 inches (76 centimeters) of rain per year.

Trees and plants thrive on the plains. Thorny shrubs and acacias cover the low, eastern plains. Baobab trees also grow in this area. These trees store water in their huge trunks and produce fruit called monkey bread. Grass covers much of the high plains in the west. Bamboo thickets and acacia groves grow near the area's rivers, including the Athi, which is one of Kenya's largest rivers.

Many animals roam the savanna. African buffalo, elephants, giraffes, rhinos, zebras, and antelopes feed on the region's tall grasses. Predators such as cheetahs, hyenas, jackals, leopards, lions, and wild dogs hunt for food in the area.

The Highlands

The highlands in central and western Kenya form a large plateau with rolling hills that covers about one-fourth of the country. This broad area of flat land is higher than the land that surrounds it. The elevation of the highlands ranges from 3,000 to 10,000 feet (914 to 3,048 meters). Nairobi, the country's capital, is located in the highlands.

▼ Long grasses, low shrubs, and short trees cover Kenya's plains.

13

The Great Rift Valley runs through the highlands. This valley begins in the Middle East and runs 4,000 miles (6,437 kilometers) south. It cuts through Kenya's highlands. The Rift contains sharp canyons and many inactive volcanoes. Mount Kenya, the country's highest point, rises just east of the Great Rift Valley.

Many lakes and waterways lie near the Great Rift Valley. The second largest freshwater lake in the world is located in the western highlands. Lake Nyanza, also called Lake Victoria, is second only to North America's Lake Superior in area. The Athi and Tana rivers flow out of the highlands.

The climate in the highlands is mild. Temperatures average 67 degrees Fahrenheit (19 degrees Celsius). The average annual rainfall in the highlands is 40 to 50 inches (102 to 127 centimeters).

The region's mild weather helps make the highlands the most fertile region in Kenya. Evergreen trees, olive trees, and bamboo thickets flourish in the region's grasslands and forests. Most of Kenya's farmland lies in this region. About 80 percent of Kenya's people, many of them farmers, make their homes here.

Many types of animals found in the plains region also live in the highlands. Eagles, monkeys, ostriches, and vultures also make the highlands their home. Crocodiles and hippos lurk in Kenya's lakes, where huge flocks of flamingos gather to eat fish.

▼ The highland region contains much of Kenya's farmland.

15

Kenya's Endangered Wildlife

Many of Kenya's large animals are endangered. Their numbers are so low that they are at risk of dying out. As Kenya's population has grown, people have turned some animal habitats into farms and livestock pastures. These changes have taken away places for wild animals to live and raise their young.

Poachers also are a threat. These people illegally hunt endangered animals for profit. Poachers kill elephants for their ivory tusks. They also kill black rhinos, the most endangered animals in Kenya, and sell their horns.

The people of Kenya are working to preserve their wildlife. Animals can live undisturbed in Kenya's national parks, including Nairobi National Park, Tsavo National Park, and Mount Kenya National Park. Cheetahs, lions, and parrots are more of Kenya's endangered wildlife that make their homes in these parks. The Kenyan government also works to prevent poachers from killing wild animals. Today, the worldwide ban on ivory sales has stopped most poaching in Kenya.

Black Rhinos

Black rhinos roam across Kenya's scrublands. Weighing up to 8,000 pounds (3,630 kilograms), rhinos are the second largest land mammals on Earth. Only elephants are larger. Black rhinos have large, powerful bodies and short, thick legs. They use their two horns to dig up bulbs for food and to fight predators.

Black rhinos usually are gentle, but they will charge when threatened. They lower their heads and run toward the enemy at up to 25 miles (40 kilometers) per hour.

Only about 2,500 black rhinos live in Africa today. Many national reserves in Africa provide places for black rhinos to live unharmed. Rhinos find plenty of food and water on the reserves.

▲ Black rhinos munch on grasses and other plants.

Fast Facts about Kenya's History

Year of founding: 1895
Founder: Great Britain
Year of independence: 1963
Constitution date: December 12, 1963
National holiday: Independence Day, December 12
Type of government: republic

Kenya's History and Government

Kenya is known as the "cradle of mankind." Some scientists think that humans first developed in Kenya. In the 1960s, scientists found bone fragments in Kenya that they believe are about 14 million years old. Some scientists say these fragments belong to the earliest ancestors of humans.

Early Inhabitants of Kenya

About 2,000 years ago, several African groups left their homelands to travel to other parts of Africa. Some of these people were looking for better land for their livestock. Others were pushed out of their crowded homelands. Three of these groups became permanent settlers of Kenya.

At about the same time, people from southwestern Asia sailed to Kenya's coast. These sailors, who were Arab, Persian, and East Indian, began trading goods

◄ Scientists like Richard Leakey work in Kenya. They have discovered bone fragments from early ancestors of humans.

▲ The Gede ruins are a popular historic site.
Arabian settlers founded the city of Gede
on Kenya's coast during the 1100s.

with the Africans in the region. By A.D. 900, Arabs had built trading posts along Kenya's coast.

The Arabs influenced coastal trade in Kenya for almost 500 years and also brought their culture and religion to the region. Called Islam, this religion is based on the teachings of the prophet Muhammad. The Arabs built large places of worship called mosques where they practiced Islam.

Arabs often married native Kenyans and combined their cultures. The African-Arabian culture became known as Swahili. The Swahili language, Kiswahili (kee-swah-HEE-lee), is a blend of African and Arabic words.

Portuguese Control

In the late 1400s, explorers from Portugal arrived on Kenya's coast in search of gold and spices. The explorers destroyed many of the Arab settlements as they searched for these riches. The Portuguese and Arabs fought for control of Kenya's coast. By the early 1500s, the Portuguese had won claim to the area.

The Portuguese traded on Kenya's coast for almost 200 years. They took Kenya's natural resources such as gold and ivory. They built an important military fort, called Fort Jesus, to protect their interests in the region. The Portuguese also tried to convert Kenyans to Christianity. Followers of this religion practice the teachings of Jesus Christ.

The Portuguese and Arabs fought for control of the fort many times. Finally, in 1729, the Arabs conquered Fort Jesus. They forced the Portuguese out and regained control of Kenya. The Arabs then controlled Kenya's coast until the 1800s.

British Rule

In the 1800s, more European explorers and traders came to Kenya. They were interested in exploring the land beyond the coast. Europeans began to claim parts of Africa for their home countries, and they began to fight over African land.

In 1884, leaders from Europe met at the Berlin Conference in Germany to divide up parts of Africa among their countries. Kenya and Uganda became part of Great Britain under the names East African Protectorate and Uganda Protectorate. The Africans did not want their land divided among the Europeans and fought to rule themselves. But the Africans were no match for the Europeans and their more advanced weapons. Defeated, the Africans in Kenya surrendered themselves to British rule.

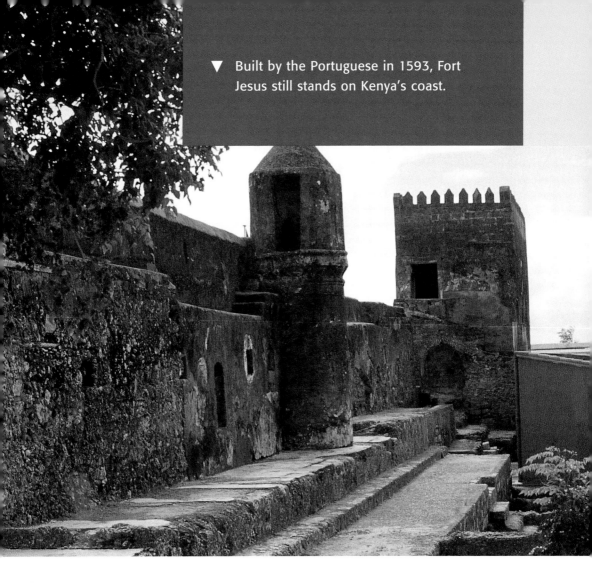

▼ Built by the Portuguese in 1593, Fort Jesus still stands on Kenya's coast.

The Mombasa-Uganda Railroad

Great Britain began to build the Mombasa-Uganda Railroad across Kenya to Uganda in 1896. The British wanted to increase trade between its East African colonies.

The railroad brought more people to the East African Protectorate. Newcomers founded the town of

Nairobi and other towns at railroad construction sites. The British government invited people from Great Britain to settle in the region to help prevent Africans from rebelling against the government. At first, many British resisted settling in the area. But some who did move to the East African Protectorate became wealthy. This opportunity for wealth drew more British people to the region.

Kenya Colony and Native Reserves

After World War I (1914–1918), many British soldiers moved to Kenya. They became farmers, planting crops and raising cattle on the fertile highlands. The British settlers drove native Africans off the good farmland and forced them to move to reserves. These areas had poorer soil and less vegetation. By 1920, so many British people had moved to Kenya that British officials made the East African Protectorate into a British colony. They named it Kenya.

British officials tried to keep the settlers and the native Africans apart. They feared the Africans would revolt against British rule. Only Africans who worked off the reserves were allowed to leave. These workers were forced to carry identity passes called kipandes.

The British restricted Africans in other ways. They did not permit Africans to enter hotels and restaurants unless they worked at these places. Africans were forced to ride in segregated train cars. Africans generally were not allowed to be in the same public places as whites.

The British government also required every African adult male to pay a tax for each hut he owned. Most African men had several wives. Each wife lived in a separate hut. Their taxes became expensive. Many African men went to work for the British government or for British landowners to pay the taxes.

▼ These Kikuyu perform a ceremony in traditional dress. The Kikuyu formed groups to ask for the return of their native land.

Fighting for Rights

The Kikuyu, a group of native Kenyans, were most affected by the British settlers. The settlers took the Kikuyu land as their own. The Kikuyu wanted their land back and were willing to fight for it.

In the early and middle 1900s, the Kikuyu formed several groups to peacefully ask for the return of their land. These groups also wanted Kenyans to have the right to vote. Voting would help the native Kenyans gain further rights.

One of these groups was the Kenyan African Union (KAU). In 1947, a Kikuyu named Jomo Kenyatta became president of the KAU. Kenyatta asked the British government to grant native Kenyans their rights. Great Britain refused.

The Mau Mau Rebellion

In the 1950s, other Kenyan political groups banded together to form a secret society called the Mau Mau (MOW MOW). The Mau Mau wanted native Kenyans to govern an independent Kenya. Members of the Mau Mau took oaths of loyalty. They promised to fight for Kenyan freedom, even if it meant killing settlers. Members of the Mau Mau attacked many British people, as well as native Kenyans who were loyal to the British government. Thirty British settlers and 30 British army soldiers died from these attacks. The British colonial powers were afraid of losing the colony and fought back with great force. The British killed about 15,000 native Kenyans.

The British government believed the KAU was leading the Mau Mau. Police arrested Kenyatta and many other political leaders. The Mau Mau Rebellion

► Jomo Kenyatta was Kenya's president for 14 years, from 1964 to 1978.

continued through 1960. The British fought back, but the Kenyan rebels remained strong.

Kenyan Independence

In 1960, government officials held a conference to give native Kenyans political power. The officials held elections to choose native Kenyan government representatives. But these representatives refused to begin work until Kenyatta was released from prison. Government officials eventually agreed to release Kenyatta.

On December 12, 1963, Kenya became independent of British rule. Leaders first made Kenya a parliamentary democracy and elected Kenyatta prime minister. Then, in 1964, the legislature made Kenya a republic and Kenyatta became Kenya's first president.

Kenyatta started to make changes in Kenya. The government purchased farmland and businesses from British settlers and returned this land to native Kenyans. Kenyatta worked to improve education and health care. He also worked to increase national pride. He told his people that different races could live together peacefully. Kenyatta's motto was "Harambee." This word, which means "pulling together," reminded people to work together to build a strong nation.

After 14 years as president, Kenyatta died in 1978. His vice president, Daniel Toroitich arap Moi, became the next president. He is a member of the Tugen (TOO-gane) ethnic group. Moi has been Kenya's president since Kenyatta's death and was last re-elected in 1997.

Kenya Today

Kenya faces many challenges today. The country's population has greatly increased, making jobs and food scarce. There are few good schools and few trained teachers. Crime and illegal drug use are common. These problems often discourage tourists from visiting Kenya, which further damages the country's economy.

In the 1990s, officials from western nations asked Kenyan officials to reform the Kenyan government. Many government politicans are corrupt. They give special favors to their friends or associates or take money illegally. The western nations threatened to withdraw financial aid if reform was not carried out. In 1991, Kenyan officials began working to stop the rapid population growth and the growing gap between the rich and poor people of the country. They also reformed policies to stop government corruption.

▲ Many children in Kenya face a life of poverty. The government is trying to stop the rapid population growth that the country faces.

▼ Kenya's National Assembly meets in Nairobi in the Parliament building.

Kenya's Government

Kenya is an independent republic. A president and a national assembly run the government. People elect the president to a five-year term. All citizens over the age of 18 can vote for the president.

Kenya's National Assembly can change the constitution and make new laws. This group has 224 members, 210 of whom are elected by citizens. The president appoints 12 of the members. The other two members are government officials who have no voting rights. The president and his appointed members hold most of the power in Kenya.

Kenya has eight provinces, including the province of Nairobi. Each province is divided into districts. Altogether, Kenya has 40 districts, each with its own government official chosen by the president. The official in each district is in charge of education, transportation, health care, public works, and other public services in the district.

Fast Facts about Kenya's Economy

Major natural resources/minerals: gold, limestone, soda ash, barium salts, and rubies

Major agricultural products: coffee, tea, corn, wheat, and sugarcane

Major types of manufactured products: batteries, cigarettes, flour, furniture, glass, plastics, soap, textiles

Major imports: machinery and transportation equipment, petroleum products, iron, and steel

Major exports: tea, coffee, horticultural products, and petroleum products

Kenya's Economy

Kenya has a workforce of about 9 million people. Most Kenyans work for themselves, farming or raising cattle to feed their families. About 20 percent of the population works for other people. The service industry provides jobs in airports, shops, hotels, restaurants, and tourist resorts. Some people find jobs in manufacturing, health care, mining, or transportation. Workers also are employed on plantations and in government jobs.

Another 6 percent of the population has jobs in small businesses. Some are fishers or taxi drivers. Street merchants sell snacks or handmade crafts. Today, more people in Kenya are operating their own small businesses. These people are called jua kalis, which means "working in the sun."

A wide gap between the wealthy and the poor exists in Kenya. A small number of Kenyans hold

◀ These women dry corn, or maize. Most of Kenya's people raise crops or cattle to feed their families.

35

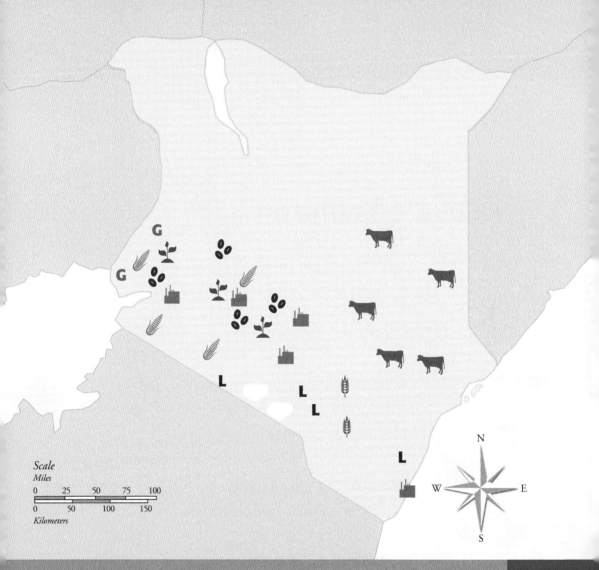

Scale
Miles

0   25   50   75   100

0   50   100   150
Kilometers

N
W   E
S

Kenya's Industries and Natural Resources

KEY

 Coffee

 Corn

G Gold

Manufacturing

L Limestone

Livestock

Soda Ash

Tea

Wheat

most of the country's wealth. They generally are powerful politicians, business associates of politicans, and owners of large plantations. About half of Kenya's population is unemployed and very poor. Some live in poor areas or slums near large cities. The uneven distribution of wealth in Kenya contributes to a high crime rate in the country.

Agriculture and Fishing

Kenya is an agricultural nation. More than three-fourths of Kenyans farm or raise livestock. Most farmers are subsistence farmers who grow crops to feed their families. Some grow a small amount of crops to sell. Farmers work small plots of land, growing maize, rice, bananas, sweet potatoes, coconuts, and millet. Maize is the most widely grown crop in Kenya.

Some Kenyans are cash-crop farmers who own large plantations with many workers. Cash crops are sold for profit and include coffee, tea, sugarcane, maize, wheat, and cotton. But most cash crops are grown on smaller farms. Kenya exports these products to countries around the world.

Some Kenyans fish in the Indian Ocean, in rivers, and on Lake Nyanza. Around Lake Nyanza, fishing is especially important because farmland is limited. These fishers catch trout, bass, and Nile perch.

Manufacturing and Mining

Kenya is one of the most industrialized countries in East Africa. About 14 percent of Kenyans work for manufacturers, mainly around the cities of Nairobi and Mombasa. Kenya's factory workers produce cement, petroleum products, chemicals, and clothing. Workers process dairy products and meat. They also make electrical equipment, motor vehicles, and textiles. Many of these goods are sold in Kenya. Others are exported to Great Britain, Germany, Tanzania, Uganda, and the United States.

Workers dig up a variety of minerals from Kenya's mines. Kenyans mine barium salts, which are used to make rubber and paint. Gold, lead, limestone, and silver also are important mineral resources. Workers mine fluorite to make chemicals and sodium carbonate for use in fire extinguishers and baking soda.

Energy and Transportation

Most energy in Kenya is provided by burning wood from the country's forests. Petroleum, hydroelectricity, and other sources provide the rest of the fuel. Kenya must import all of the petroleum it uses.

Kenyans often travel by bus, taxi, or plane because most do not own their own cars. Cars can travel across

Kenya's Money

Kenya's unit of currency is the Kenyan shilling (KSh). One Kenyan shilling equals 100 Kenyan cents. Currency exchange rates change every day. In the early 2000s, about 78 Kenyan shillings equaled 1 U.S. dollar, and about 51 Kenyan shillings equaled 1 Canadian dollar.

1 shilling coin

50 cent piece

10 shilling bill (front)

50 shilling bill (front)

10 shilling coin

50 shilling bill (back)

almost 30,000 miles (48,279 kilometers) of roads, 2,400 miles (3,862 kilometers) of which are paved. More than 1,000 miles (1,600 kilometers) of railroad tracks also cross the country. The cities of Nairobi and Mombasa have international airports, while Kisumu and Malindi have smaller airports.

Tourism

The tourism industry is an important part of Kenya's economy. Many people visit Kenya each year to watch and photograph wildlife or vacation on beaches. Most of these people are from Europe, and about 10 percent are from the United States. In recent years, tourism brought more than $200 million (about $290 million Canadian) into Kenya each year.

Kenya's tourism industry declined in the 1990s. Foreigners heard about widespread crime, disease, and ethnic clashes in the country. These problems kept many people from taking trips to Kenya.

▲ These tourists met a cheetah during a
photo safari to Kenya. The country's
wildlife attracts many tourists.

Fast Facts about Kenya's People

Population distribution: urban, 20 percent; rural, 80 percent

Official languages: Kiswahili and English

Population growth rate: 1.53 percent

Life expectancy: 48 years

Literacy rate: 78 percent of the population over age 15 can read

Traditional foods: beans, chapati, fish, rice, ugali

People, Culture, and Daily Life

Today, more than 40 ethnic groups live in Kenya. Each of these groups descended from one of the country's first three ethnic groups—the Bantu, the Nilotic, or the Cushitic. Today's ethnic groups often are identified with the three larger groups.

The Bantu people are the largest group in Kenya. They make up 59 percent of the country's population. The Bantu originally may have migrated from West Africa to Kenya. Today, the Bantu people live in three general regions—the Lake Nyanza area, central Kenya, and the southern coastal region. Bantu groups include the Kikuyu, Luhya, Meru, and Mijikenda peoples.

The Nilotic people are the second largest group in Kenya. They originally lived near the Nile River in north-central Africa. Nilotic people now make their homes around Lake Nyanza and in the Great Rift

◄ These schoolchildren are Kikuyu, just one of more than 40 ethnic groups in Kenya.

Valley of western Kenya. Nilotic groups include the Luo, Maasai, Samburu, and Turkana peoples.

The Cushitic people are the smallest group in Kenya. They live in the north, where they herd camels and sheep. Cushitic groups include the Boran and the Galla.

Major Ethnic Groups

With about 6 million people, the Kikuyu people are the largest and most powerful ethnic group in Kenya. As part of the larger Bantu group, the Kikuyu people are among the nation's richest and best-educated groups. They often hold important government positions. The Kikuyu live on some of Kenya's most fertile land in the highlands near Mount Kenya. Many Kikuyu people are farmers who raise vegetables and cattle for their families and grow coffee to sell.

The Luo (LOO-oh) ethnic group is Kenya's second most powerful group. About 4 million people are Luo. Their land extends from the shores of Lake Nyanza inland to southwestern Kenya. Most Luo women grow crops and raise livestock. Luo men often work as fishers, shopkeepers, mechanics, or machinists. The Luo hold many of the skilled jobs in Kenya.

The Maasai (mah-SYE) ethnic group is among the best known in Kenya. This group has fewer than one

▼ Maasai women wear traditional jewelry. They add to their jewelry as they grow older.

million people—less than 2 percent of Kenya's population. But the Maasai have a reputation for being brave hunters and fierce warriors. They live in the Great Rift Valley of western Kenya. Many Maasai dress in traditional clothing and practice their original customs. They live almost entirely by hunting and herding. The Maasai are nomads who move often to find fresh grassland for their cattle.

These boys and many other Kenyans have put aside their traditional clothing for more modern dress.

A Changing Lifestyle

Kenya's ethnic groups are changing. More and more Kenyans are moving to large cities and shedding their traditional ways of life. They put aside their traditional clothing in favor of more modern styles. Rural men often must travel to cities to find jobs. They work away from home for months at a time, leaving their wives to care for their families and raise crops by themselves. These changes have led to weaker ties within families and ethnic groups.

For some ethnic groups, the family structure has greatly changed. In the past, it was customary for Kenyan men to have more than one wife. Wealthy men may have had five or six wives. The men divided their time among these wives and their families. In recent years, this practice has become less common. Kenya's Christians speak out against it. Most Kenyan men also cannot afford to support more than one family.

Women in Kenya

Most Kenyan women, like many men, do not hold paying jobs. Women often care for children and help raise livestock. They also grow crops and build and repair family homes. Many women carry food and other goods to markets to sell or trade. Some women

▼ A Kenyan family poses outside their rural home.
Many rural homes do not have electricity or
other modern conveniences.

work outside their homes, holding jobs as nurses,
teachers, or bankers. Most women with paying jobs
live in large cities.

In the past, Kenyan women had few rights. Most
women could not own land. For many years, girls
were not allowed to attend school. But this situation is
changing. Women own land, and girls now go to

school and receive training for jobs. A few women have been elected to the National Assembly. The National Woman's Council of Kenya teaches women job skills. This organization also gives business loans to women and works for more women's rights.

Cities and Villages

Kenyan cities are important centers for business and tourism. City dwellers often live in apartments. Other people make their homes in crowded communities on the outskirts of cities.

Many ethnic groups in Kenya live in small, rural villages. Kenyan villages often have a few shops and hold an outdoor market once a week. A village usually contains people from a single ethnic group. Families share farmland in these villages. Homes often do not have electricity, plumbing, or other modern conveniences.

Education

Although attending school is not required for Kenyan children, most attend elementary school for four years. Their schooling is free during these years. Family members must pay for their children's education for the remaining three years of elementary school and any additional schooling. Most Kenyan children

Learn to Speak Kiswahili

The more than 40 different ethnic groups in Kenya each have their own language. In the 1800s, trade caravans that spoke Kiswahili came from the coast and introduced their language to the groups. When the British arrived, they decided to use Kiswahili as the language of government. Missionaries taught English as a foreign language. Kenya's national languages now are English and Kiswahili. Some Kiswahili words appear below.

hello—jambo (JAHM-bo)
goodbye—kwa heri (KWAH Harry)
please—tafadhali (tah-fah-THAHL-ee)
thank you—asante (ah-SAN-tay)
Do you speak English?—
Unasungumoca Kiingerea?
(OO-na-SUN-goo-mo-za Kin-GAR-eza)

▲ Kenyan schoolchildren learn both English and Kiswahili.

attend school for at least a few years. This practice accounts for Kenya's 78 percent literacy rate. School subjects are taught in English. But schoolchildren also learn to read and write Kiswahili. Eighty percent of Kenyan children receive at least an elementary education.

Kenyan cities have many schools, but Kenyan villages often have only one school. Kenya also has a shortage of secondary schools, especially in isolated or rural areas. Communities have set up harambee schools in some of these areas. The community pays for the school without government help and community children can attend.

Religion

Kenya's constitution grants freedom of worship. People of any religion can live and practice their religion in Kenya. Most Kenyans are Christians who follow the Protestant or Catholic faiths. Muslims in Kenya practice the religion of Islam. Many Kenyans also practice their traditional tribal religions.

Most Kenyans blend Christianity with local traditions. They believe in lesser gods that control events such as rain, dry spells, crop growth, and the health of children. Kenyans believe these gods live in trees, rivers, caves, and other places in nature.

Food

Kenyan foods vary from region to region and among ethnic groups. In cities, East Indian foods are popular. Some favorite Kenyan dishes are ugali, beans, spiced beef and rice, and samozas. A samoza is dough wrapped around a filling of diced cooked potatoes, onions, carrots, and spices. People eat samozas as a snack or an appetizer.

Rural Kenyans usually eat traditional foods. Herders often drink cattle blood mixed with milk. Farmers eat cereal dishes as well as fruits and vegetables from their fields. Both herders and farmers eat meat on special occasions.

Arts and Literature

Kenya has many talented artists. Wood carvers and sculptors in Kenya make good-luck charms, masks, and wooden figures. African art is displayed and admired all around the world.

Traditional literature in Kenya consists of folktales. Mothers often sing or recite stories to their children about monsters, witches, wizards, spirits, and talking animals. Many Kenyan writers now write modern literature. Ngugi wa Thiong'o, one of Kenya's most famous writers, is known worldwide for his novels and essays.

Make Ugali

Ugali is a popular dish in Kenya. Almost all ethnic groups in Kenya eat some form of ugali.

What You Need

4 cups (1000 mL) water
saucepan with cover
2 cups (500 mL) maize
(white corn flour)
wooden stirring spoon
salt (optional)
measuring cups
plate

What You Do

1. Bring 4 cups (1000 mL) water to boil in saucepan.
2. Reduce heat to medium.
3. Add 2 cups (500 mL) maize gradually, stirring until the consistency is stiff.
4. Cover for about 5 minutes, stirring occasionally.
5. Stir again and form into a mound.
6. The ugali will be done when it pulls from the sides of the pan easily and does not stick.
7. Cover the pot with a plate and tip the pan over so that the ugali drops on the plate.
8. Add salt to taste.
9. Serve in flat slabs with meat stew.

Makes 10 servings

▲ Uhuru park offers a view of the Nairobi skyline. Residents gather here to play games and paddle boats on the park's pond.

Sports and Recreation

Kenyans enjoy watching and playing many sports. Popular sports include boxing, hockey, horseback riding, tennis, and volleyball. Major sporting events take place in Kenya's cities. Soccer, which is called football in Kenya, is the country's favorite sport. Kenya has a national soccer team. Track and field events also are popular in Kenya. Kenya's world-class runners have won many Olympic medals.

The British colonists brought some sports to Kenya, many of which stayed and became popular with Kenyans. Some of these sports include cricket, rugby, golf, and polo.

Kenyan Holidays

Kenya has many national and religious holidays that both locals and tourists enjoy. Eid-al-Fitr occurs after Ramadan. This day celebrates the end of the Muslim month of fasting. People put on brightly colored new clothes and participate in street festivals.

Kenyans celebrate two main national holidays. Janhuri, Kenya's Independence Day, is celebrated on December 12. Another national holiday is Kenyatta Day on October 20. This day is the anniversary of Jomo Kenyatta's arrest by the British in 1952. Kenyatta Day reminds Kenyans of how hard they fought for their independence.

▲ These Kenyan children play soccer,
Kenya's national sport.

Kenya's National Symbols

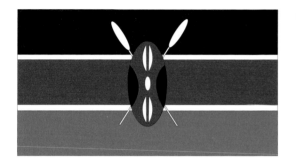

◀ Kenya's Flag

The Kenyan flag was adopted in 1963, when Kenya became an independent country. The black stripe represents the Kenyan people. The red stripe stands for the blood Kenyans shed in the fight for independence. The green stripe represents the fertile land of Kenya. The two white stripes stand for peace and harmony. The war shield and two spears symbolize Kenya's pride, traditions, and defense of freedom.

◀ Kenya's Coat of Arms

Kenya's coat of arms is the symbol of Kenya's ruling political party, the Kenya African National Union. The word "Harambee" appears beneath the war shield. This word means "pulling together" in Kiswahili.

Other National Symbols

National anthem—"Anthem of the Nation"
National sport—soccer
National dish—ugali
National motto—Harambee

Timeline

1690s to mid-1700s
Arabians drive out the Portuguese and take control of Kenya.

A.D. 900
Arabian merchants build outposts along the Kenyan coast.

1884
Britain takes control of Kenya and names it the East African Protectorate.

B.C.   A.D.   1700   1800

Prehistoric times to A.D. 1500
People migrate to Kenya from all around Africa.

1498
The Portuguese arrive at Mombasa; they take control of Kenya's coast and later build Fort Jesus.

1840s–1850s
The first British missionaries and explorers arrive in Kenya.

1903
The first British settlers arrive; they drive native Kenyans off their land.

1904
Britain abolishes slavery in Kenya.

1947
The Kenya African Union (KAU) is formed to drive out the British; Jomo Kenyatta becomes president of the KAU.

1963
Kenya gains its independence and becomes a parliamentary democracy.

1964
Kenya becomes a republic.

1997
Moi is re-elected as president.

1900   **1950**   **2000**

1920
Britain makes Kenya a British colony and names it Kenya Colony.

1952 to 1960
Mau Mau uprisings occur.

1978
Jomo Kenyatta dies. Vice president Daniel Toroitich arap Moi becomes president.

Words to Know

corruption (kuh-RUHP-shuhn)—bribery or other reasons to do what is illegal or immoral

endangered (en-DAYN-jurd)—in danger of becoming extinct

lagoon (luh-GOON)—a shallow pool of water separated from the ocean by a narrow strip of land

mosque (MOSK)—a building used by Muslims for worship; Arabs built many mosques along Kenya's coast.

nomad (NOH-mad)—someone who moves around instead of living in one place; Kenyan nomads often travel to find grasslands and water for their cattle.

plateau (pla-TOH)—an area of high, flat land

poacher (POHCH-ur)—a person who hunts or fishes illegally

reserve (ri-ZURV)—an area of land set aside by the government for a specific purpose; the British government forced native Kenyans to live on reserves.

savanna (suh-VAN-uh)—a flat, grassy plain with few or no trees found in tropical areas

segregation (seg-ruh-GAY-shuhn)—the practice of keeping people or things apart from another group; Kenyans were segregated during the British rule of Kenya.

To Learn More

Derr, Victoria. *Kenya.* Countries of the World. Milwaukee: Gareth Stevens Publishing, 1999.

McCollum, Sean. *Kenya.* Globe-Trotters Club. Minneapolis: Carolrhoda Books, 1999.

McNair, Sylvia, and Lynne Mansure. *Kenya.* Enchantment of the World Second Series. New York: Children's Press, 2001.

McQuail, Lisa. *The Masai of East Africa.* First Peoples. Minneapolis: Lerner Publications, 2002.

Ridgeway, Rick. *The Shadow of Kilimanjaro: On Foot across East Africa.* New York: Henry Holt and Company, 1998.

Useful Addresses

Embassy of the Republic of Kenya

2249 R Street NW

Washington, DC 20008

Embassy of the Republic of Kenya in Canada

415 Laurier Street West

Ottawa, ON K1N 5A6

Canada

Internet Sites

Africa Online—Kenya

http://www.africaonline.com/site/ke/index.jsp

Varied information and links about Kenya

CIA—The World Factbook 2000—Kenya

http://www.cia.gov/cia/publications/factbook/geos/ke.html

Good information from the U.S. Central Intelligence Agency

KenyaWeb

http://www.Kenyaweb.com

Large resource covering history, culture, and other information

The Kenyan Embassy in Washington, DC

http://www.kenyaembassy.com

Travel and business information about Kenya

▲ Flamingos are found along Kenya's lakes and coasts.

Index